Brown girl
Brown boy
What could you be?

by
Dr. Temika S. Edwards

Illustrated by Pearly L.

JUDGE

Published by FIT2LEAD Publishing

Dedicated to
all the brown girls and boys
who aspire to be what they want
to be and beyond. Including my little
brown boy and brown girl,
Kristian and Trevor Jr.

Brown Girl
Brown Boy
What could you be?

I could be an
Airline Pilot.
Watch, you will see.

Pilots are the drivers of airplanes and
helicopters. They can fly people and goods from
one place to another place.

Brown Girl
Brown Boy
What else could you be?

I could be an
Astronaut.
Watch,
you will see.

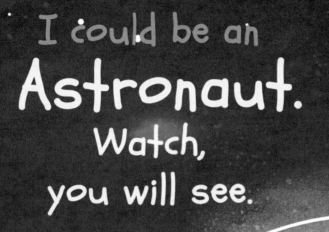

Astronauts travel in spacecrafts into space. Some Astronauts have even walked on the moon!

Brown Girl
Brown Boy
What else could you be?

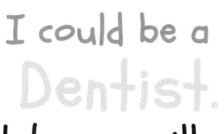

I could be a
Dentist.

Watch, you will see.

Dentists are like doctors for our teeth.
They fix cavities and remove tooth
decay. They treat diseases of the mouth
as well and teach people how to look
after their teeth properly.

Brown Girl
Brown Boy
What else could you be?

I could be a
Doctor.
Watch, you will see.

Doctors help to heal sick people. Some doctors examine patients and give them medicine. Some doctors operate on people.

Brown Girl
Brown Boy
What else could you be?

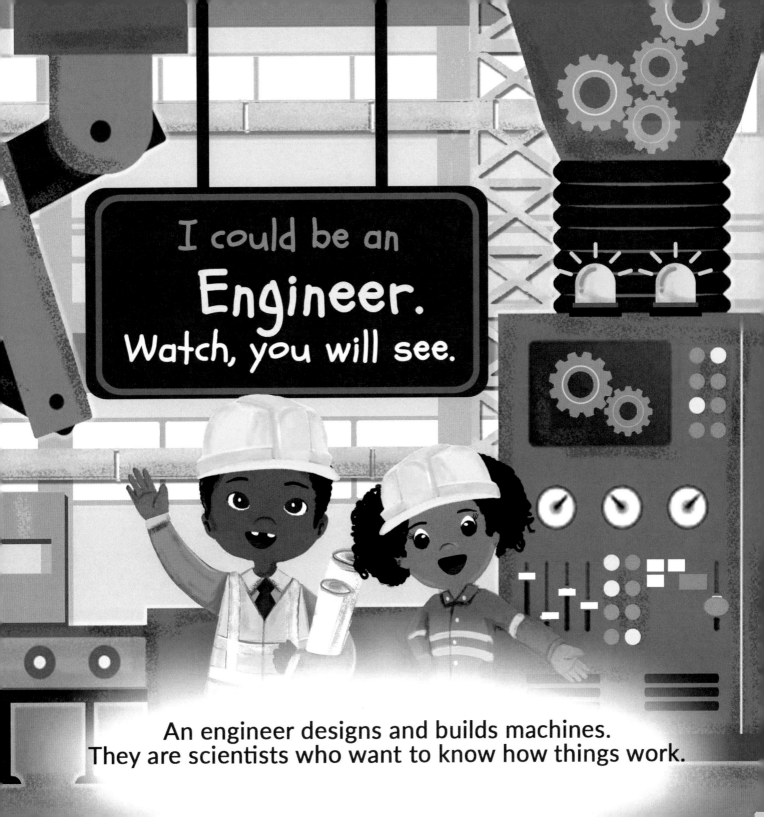

I could be an **Engineer.**
Watch, you will see.

An engineer designs and builds machines.
They are scientists who want to know how things work.

I could be a Financial Advisor.
Watch, you will see.

A financial advisor helps people to manage their money, and helps them to make good financial decisions.

Brown Girl
Brown Boy
What else could you be?

I could be a
Judge.
Watch, you will see.

JUDGE

A judge is a person who is in control of a court of law. It is their duty to conduct trials fairly and to follow the laws of the state and the United States of America.

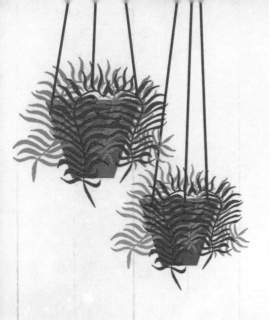

Brown Girl
Brown Boy
What else could you be?

Brown Girl
Brown Boy
What else could you be?

I could be an
Scientist.

Watch, you will see.

Scientists observe things. Scientists use their senses when solving problems. They use their eyes to spot details. They use their noses to detect if something is stinky. They use their hearing, touch, and even sense of taste. Scientists measure things. Scientists use scales, rulers, thermometers, and lots of other tools to measure things. Scientists communicate their findings. They tell other people about their discoveries. It can be in the local news or in a science book.

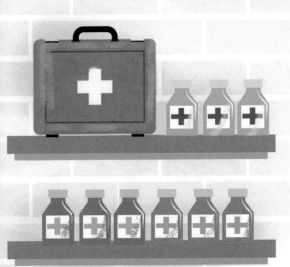

Brown Girl
Brown Boy
What else could you be?

I could be a

Veterinarian.

Watch, you will see.

A veterinarian is an animal doctor. They can help to heal all sorts of animals, from mice to elephants. In certain situations, vets can have very dangerous jobs!

Brown Girl
Brown Boy
What else could you be?

I could be the
President or
Vice President
of United States.

Watch, you will see.

The President is both the head of state and head of government of the United States of America, and Commander-in-Chief of the armed forces. Under Article II of the Constitution, the President is responsible for the execution and enforcement of the laws created by Congress.

The Vice President is usually seen as an integral part of a president's administration and presides over the Senate only on ceremonial occasions or when a tie-breaking vote may be needed. The VP is a key presidential advisor, governing partner, and representative of the president.

I could be an

Airline Pilot, Astronaut,

Dentist, Doctor,

Engineer, Financial Advisor,

Judge, Psychologist,

Scientist, Veterinarian,

President or Vice President
of United States of America.

I can be
ANYTHING I WANT
TO BE.
Watch, you will see.

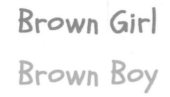

Brown Girl

Brown Boy

We know what you are and what you could be.

You are wonderfully and marvelously made.

You are brave, strong and smart.

You can be a record breaker, rule maker,
leading the next generation of leaders.

You can be
ANYTHING
you want to be.
Believing is key.
Watch, you will see.

There are many different professions
that you could be, because

I see GREATNESS
looking back at me.

Made in the USA
Middletown, DE
07 August 2021